PICTURES OF TRADITIONAL JEWISH FAMILY LIFE

LIBRARY OF JEWISH ART

Edited by

JOSEPH GUTMANN
Professor of Art History
Wayne State University

PICTURES OF
TRADITIONAL JEWISH
FAMILY LIFE

By
MORITZ DANIEL OPPENHEIM

With an Introduction by
ALFRED WERNER

KTAV PUBLISHING HOUSE, INC.
NEW YORK
1976

Library of Congress Cataloging in Publication Data

Oppenheim, Moritz, d. 1882.
   Pictures of traditional Jewish family life.

   (The Library of Jewish art)
   Translation of Bilder aus dem altjüdischen Familienleben.
   1. Oppenheim, Moritz, d. 1882. 2. Jewish way of life
in art. I. Title.
ND588.058A4313   759.3   76-41250
ISBN 0-87068-472-8

TABLE OF CONTENTS

To my wife Lisa Werner

OPPENHEIM: A REDISCOVERED MASTER

by Alfred Werner

I

The late Professor Franz Landsberger drew attention to a theme that frequently occupied nineteenth-century Jewish painters: present-day Jewish life. The pictures produced were "pleasing and friendly, corresponding to the comfort and peace in which the Jews lived at the height of the Emancipation." He then mentioned the most popular of these genre-painters, Moritz Daniel Oppenheim, giving the year 1800 as the one in which he saw the light of the world (*A History of Jewish Art*). The painter himself was not so sure about this date. All he had been told, he wrote in his charming little book of reminiscences, *Erinnerungen*, published posthumously, was that his pious mother had given birth to him after having

9

fasted on that minor holiday, the 10th of Tevet. But was it in 1799, 1800, or 1801? At that time, no registers of Jewish births were kept.

In any event, the locale into which the infant was born was the *Judengasse* of Hanau, a town fourteen miles east of Frankfort-on-Main, Germany (a commercial and industrial center, it played a role in medieval as well as early modern Jewish history). Around 1800, the *kehillah* numbered about five hundred souls and had its own synagogue, cemetery, bakery, slaughterhouse, hospital, and shelter for the homeless. It even provided its own night-watchman and fire-engine.

Moritz was born in time to enjoy the fruits of the French Revolution. Napoleon's soldiers, who occupied Hanau in 1806, carried at least some of the progressive principles of this revolution into a defeated reactionary Germany. Hanau was incorporated in 1810 into the Grand Duchy of Frankfort, whose new constitution decreed "that all Jews living in Frankfort . . . together with their children and descendants, should enjoy civil rights and privileges equal to other citizens."

The boy attended the local one-room Talmud Torah (whose pupils had to bring their own candles and firewood) but also, in the Christian part of the town, *Schoenschreibeunterricht* (instruction in German penmanship), enduring the molestation of his Gentile classmates. Under the changed political circumstances he was also able to enroll at the secular *Gymnasium* (the secondary school where Latin and Greek were among the subjects taught). He was not an attentive student of the humanities, though. Inexplicably, he yearned to become an artist (no Jewish youngster he knew had any desire to be one). Luckily, his parents, though neither rich nor sophisticated, let him, who was so different from their other children, devote more and more of his time away from conventional studies to drawing and painting at the town's *Zeichenakademie* (Academy of Drawing).

To judge by Oppenheim's earliest surviving works, instruction there must have been solid and serious, even if confined to the exact translation of three-dimensional objects—mostly plaster casts of antique busts—onto the two-dimensionality of paper. At one point Moritz used his own works to decorate the family *sukkah!* Undoubtedly, he had a precocious talent, for he was only fourteen when the Academy's director recommended him to an aristocratic collector who owned works by Old Masters. Moritz was hired to make copies of some of these pictures. Still thinking of himself as an *armer Judenjunge* (poor Jewish youth), he was embarrassed upon being invited by the high-born couple to lunch at their castle. He could not bring himself to eat anything, though he had been assured that the food served him had been prepared by a Jew, in strict accord with the laws of *kashrut*.

Provincial Hanau was soon exchanged for the more cosmopolitan Munich, where Moritz enthusiastically studied at the Academy and also learned the relatively new craft of "lithography." However, he yearned to proceed to the *Weltstadt* (metropolis) Paris. Arriving there at nineteen, he chose to study under the famous old Jean-Baptiste Regnault, who specialized in antique subject matter. Apparently, he took no interest in his own coevals, the romantic daredevils Géricault and Delacroix, who are not even mentioned at all in *Erinnerungen*.

From Paris, Oppenheim went on to Rome, where he spent four years. Even away from home, he remained an orthodox Jew who took his meals in the Ghetto whenever possible, and whom "the pomp of St. Peter's" impressed as "an exhibition calculated upon effect in contrast to the unpretentiousness and proud simplicity of the Jewish synagogue." Nevertheless, he was on intimate terms with the "Nazarenes," a group of fervently Catholic Germans who had established themselves in an abandoned monastery and whose program was the revival of Christian art by emulating the naive and simple, yet ardently religious, pictures of pre-Renaissance masters. Among his friends was Philipp Veit, a Nazarene of distinguished Jewish ancestry—one of his grandfathers was the celebrated philosopher, Moses Mendelssohn.

Curiously, in Rome Oppenheim drew and painted, along with episodes taken from the Hebrew Bible, scenes from the New Testament—like any good Nazarene. Competing anonymously for a prize to be awarded by the Accademia San Lucca, he made a drawing in 1823, *Christ and the Samaritan Woman at the Well*. It was considered the best in the competition—until it was discovered by the jury that the artist was German, and a Jew at that. When the award was withheld from him, one of the jurors, the Danish sculptor Bertel Thorwaldsen, took his part; if he failed in his efforts to have Oppenheim obtain what he deserved, the unbiased Thorwaldsen at least managed to ensure that nobody else received the prize.

By 1825, Oppenheim had become tired of living abroad. He returned to Germany, to settle in Frankfort for the rest of his long, fruitful life, interrupted only now and then by travel to some of the major European cities. He was kept busy by a steady stream of lucrative portrait commissions. A charming, friendly man, with a good sense of humor, who never made an enemy, he was the epitome of the law-abiding solid citizen. He married his childhood sweetheart, Adelheid Cleve, who bore him three children. After her death, he remarried, and three children also resulted from this second union. He was only mildly interested in politics, and the changes in aesthetics—effected by Romantics, Realists, Impressionists—had no impact upon him. A conscientious picture-maker, he fully enjoyed the good life he lived, and with naive pleasure he related, at eighty, that he had come to be known as "Rothschild among the painters," as well as "painter of the Rothschilds." Concerning the latter, he recalled:

". . . I had much to do for the Rothschild family; the branch which had been settled in Naples resettled here [in Frankfort]; they, as well as Baron Anselm [a grandson of the dynasty's founder] with his art-loving wife, Charlotte, established princely households. I attended the most eminent and most dazzling social gatherings. When I was presented to the Baroness Charlotte, she asked whether I would give her instruction. I answered that customarily I did not impart instruction, but that I would be at her service gladly and entirely. Noticing the haughtiness which shone through these words, she responded, 'Baron Gérard [the official portraitist of the Bonaparte family] has also instructed me, and I paid him for each lesson a louis d'or.'

"This annoyed me a little; nevertheless, I repeated only that I would be entirely at her service. As a matter of fact, unlike other teachers, I did not give her appointments for specific hours; instead, from the beginning I accustomed her to my irregular comings and goings. Nevertheless, she was very satisfied with her teacher, as proved by her frequent visits to my studio and by her amiable little letters in French. . . . She also had me decorate the cupola of her house; I painted mythological subjects in the eight panels. I presented her as Psyche without telling her; but she soon noticed it. On special occasions I composed poems for her. However, the culmination of my instruction came when she illustrated a Haggadah for her uncle Amschel.

"I designed the subjects for it, which she carried out in the style of the old missals. To this end she obtained from Paris, not without considerable expense, manuscripts illuminated with miniatures. Messeritz, at that time the best Jewish calligrapher, inscribed the text, and this manuscript certainly cost the Baroness several thousand Gulden. . . ."

During his lifetime, Oppenheim was showered with honors. He made ample use of the "Professor honoris causa" title bestowed upon him at Weimar by the Grand Duke at the prompting of Goethe (back home, he reciprocated by making illustrations for the great poet's *Hermann und Dorothea*, an idyllic love story, set in a peaceful, simple German village yet phrased in classic hexameters). He was more amused than angered when one of Frankfort's Jewish bankers thus introduced him to a group of military men, "Herr Professor Oppenheim, ein Maler—hat's aber gottlob nicht noetig!" (i.e.: he paints—but, thank God, he doesn't have to).

Indeed, he had accumulated enough wealth to afford to retire from painting. This, of course, he never did—hours before his death in 1882, he started a picture, a *Finding of Moses* (a repetition of a picture made in 1833). For more than sixty years he worked methodically, systematically, without any leisure or diversions, without any of the exciting but often perilous extracurricular activities usually associated, in the popular mind, with an artist's life. He painted doggedly, indefatigably. He was commissioned to paint imaginary portraits of long defunct German emperors (for the "Roemer," Frankfort's old city hall), and an endless series of pictures illustrating literary, historical, or religious scenes that were well received by the public and often acquired by German museums. Many celebrities sat for him. The one best known all over the world was the poet Heinrich Heine, painted in 1831. No two persons were ever as dissimilar as these two. Yet Oppenheim, the solid bourgeois, somehow managed to penetrate into the psyche of this uncommon writer, perpetuating for posterity his ironical and even cynical outlook on life.

II

Oppenheim is now best remembered on account of his cycle of genre paintings, *Bilder aus dem altjuedischen Familienleben*, literally, "Pictures of Old-Time Jewish Family Life," though "traditional" might be a better translation than "Old-Time." At any rate, to him goes the honor of having been the earliest Jewish professional artist to occupy himself with the rendering of Jewish life in the synagogue or home, at religious ceremonies or in enjoyment of simple pleasures. Most of these oils, painted between ca. 1865 and 1880, and made popular through black-and-white photographic reproductions, issued in albums, seem like old theatre or movie stills: each actor is made-up, costumed and posed carefully, with the minimum of facial expression that the role requires.

But his nineteenth-century audiences liked them very much, especially those who still adhered to the Jewish religion, and to the traditional style of life, but were to find that assimilation and progress were making it more and more difficult to follow the multitude of detailed observances with the required strictness. At the same time, they liked Oppenheim's general attitude to religion and life, which was not forbiddingly moralistic, and his ability to sweeten religion by giving the scene, occasionally, a slightly amusing slant. Altogether, the pictures have, despite their "educational" purpose, a warmth of understanding, a humanity, missing from the more mechanically manufactured products of those genre painters who were Oppenheim's contemporaries.

He began the series with a picture which, oddly, is now the last (plate 20) in this volume. Like other story-telling pictures of the period, this plate 20 has a long explanatory title, *The Return of a Jewish Volunteer from the Wars of Liberation to His Family Still Living in Accordance to Old Rites* (though the title is often abbreviated so as to consist of the first six words).

Painted in 1833 or 1834, it was bought by a group of "Israelite citizens" of the Grand Duchy of Baden, and presented to Gabriel Riesser the most eloquent spokesman of German Jewry in the fight for full emancipation (because of his Jewish faith, he had been rejected as a lecturer by Heidelberg University, and in Hamburg he was barred from the practice of law). Riesser, acknowledging the gift, stated the "generation gap" the picture alludes to: "The father is foolish who wishes to wrap his son in the garments of antiquity, but lacking in dignity is the son ashamed of his father, the generation ashamed of its past."

The conflict is obvious: the wounded young officer appears to have arrived at his parental home on a Saturday afternoon, and to have violated the injunction against traveling on Shabbat. He also wears a military decoration in the shape of a cross—and his pious father examines it with a pride that is mixed with uneasiness.

But it was important that the picture pointed at a fact often denied by the enemies of Jewish emancipation—that the Jew could be as patriotic as his Christian fellow-townsman. Indeed, in the 1813-1815 War of Liberation which led to Napoleon's defeat, hundreds of Prussian Jews participated as volunteers; many of them received high decorations for bravery; some were wounded, or even killed. Graphically supporting the arguments of those who advocated full civil rights for Jews, *The Return* made a timely appearance at a moment when the enfranchisement of German Jews was vigorously debated in public.

Between 1834, when *The Return* was finished, and the continuation with *Ushering in the Sabbath* (plate 7), three decades were to elapse. More and more pictures, conceived in that spirit, were to come. A Frankfort publisher felt that, having a mass appeal, the pictures ought to be circulated as photographic prints. Since nineteenth-century photography was not yet able to reproduce the color values of a painting, the artist did them over, with slight changes, as *grisailles*—gray monochrome oils. From six the series increased to twenty. There were inexpensive editions in small format as well as mammoth "coffee table" books placed centrally in Jewish homes, as status symbols, but also, perhaps, as demonstrations of pride in one's Jewish ancestry, for all Christian visitors to see. A few lucky ones, who were sufficiently wealthy, bought the originals—those in colors, as well as the *grisailles*, and whatever replicas the artist was accommodating enough to make.

His pictures are, undeniably, didactic, but in a way to give, through warmth and joyfulness, a certain pleasure to the beholder (significantly, scenes showing people on sickbeds and portrayals of funerals or burials are carefully avoided). To the honor of the master it must be said that, unlike so many of his imitators, he took his task very seriously. All of the pictures are painted with finicky meticulousness; at the same time, Oppenheim was too good an artist to permit preoccupation with detail to detract from the solidity of design, from the completeness to the over-all concept.

The nostalgic note is enhanced by the fact that all figures (except for the German soldiers and officers on plate 19) are made to wear "historical" costumes rather than those of the period in which the albums were issued—the men, for instance, are clad in the knee-breeches, three-cornered hats and buckled shoes of the late Rococo instead of nineteenth-century pantaloons. As might be expected, the Jews—there are, apparently, no Gentiles present, except for the maids carrying dishes, or, from a distance, watching some of the strange proceedings—are nearly always decked out in their Sabbath best, their bodies and even their souls washed clean. The peddler who, leaving his home for his trade routes, puts his hand on the *mezuzah*, looks reasonably well groomed. This is even true of the beggar (possibly a Gentile) in the same picture (plate 18). Whenever this is feasible, the emphasis is on the exterior—the women's silken gowns, the furniture, the ritual objects, and on the various light effects. By contrast, not enough effort was made to distinguish these good folks too much from one another in feature and expression.

Nevertheless, Oppenheim gave us authentic types, grouped with an artful plausibility, the figures strongly modeled in fresh colors. His men, women and children may be a bit stiff and stuffy, and even the above-mentioned beggar outside the home of the very unproletarian peddler looks and acts with astonishing decorum. But Oppenheim does not always beautify—the old grandma is an old grandma, and the middle-aged fathers, or grandfathers, have enormous pot-bellies.

In the present album—the facsimile reproduction is based on one originally issued decades ago—the cycle starts with *The*

Child Entering the Covenant. The *Brit-Milah* is about to take place. The godmother brings the infant to the door of the synagogue, where the godfather and the *mohel* are already present. The lady does not dare to enter the room. For in Oppenheim's Frankfort, women did not participate in any ritual functions within the house of orthodox worship. They were merely passive spectators in the gallery—they appear partially hidden behind the lattice work, which allows them just a glimpse of what is happening on the floor of the synagogue (plate 2). Even when, in the large living room, the thirteen-year-old delivers his *bar mitzvah* discourse, the only female present is the mother (plate 5).

This mother, as well as her daughters, turn up, of course, at all festivals at home, for instance, at the Passover and Sukkot meals. But, as a rule, what is depicted is a man's world. Men, wearing skullcaps and *talletim* at prayer. Or, informally, on Hanukkah, playing chess in one room, cards in the adjoining room. Everybody seems to be well off. The old Frankfort synagogue is furnished with fine ceremonial objects; it is spacious, and so very unlike the simple *shuls* in the ghetto of Rome that Oppenheim had admired as a young art student. In the home, too, the ceremonial objects seem to be costly. Goblets, table cloth, carpet and furniture are excellent. Books in good binding are everywhere. There are even pictures on the walls.

It was customary for Jews to be good patriotic Germans. In plate 5 a likeness of Prussia's King Frederick the Great can be seen on a wall. If plate 20 refers to the Wars of Liberation, plate 19 takes us to the time of the Franco-Prussian War of 1870–1871. In a shell-torn room, somewhere in France, ten German-Jewish soldiers and officers, wearing helmets or military caps, have formed the required *minyan*. A significant detail: the large cross on the wall is covered with a shawl.

The most popular pictures seem to be *The Wedding* and *Ushering in the Sabbath*, as they are reproduced in nearly all histories of Jewish art, and in Jewish·encyclopedias. Unfortunately, very few of the original oils of the series appear to have survived, and even of the twenty *grisailles* only half the number are still in existence. But a few albums can still be found in some major libraries, and the present reprint of the series will take Oppenheim's message to many American Jews who will find it pleasurable, as well as informative, to look at Oppenheim's pictures.

Admittedly, he was not a pathfinder in the realm of modern aesthetics, and his niche in art history is not a big one. But he was an honest man and a sincere painter, endowed with considerable skills. He certainly deserves a good spot in Jewish *Kulturgeschichte* (cultural history)—and in our hearts. For the life he so charmingly depicted in his anecdotal work came to a sudden halt when the Nazis destroyed every vestige of German-Jewish symbiosis over a thousand-year period.

1 THE CHILD ENTERS THE COVENANT

Brit-Milah, the covenant of circumcision, is the ceremony of cutting away the foreskin (it is often called "the covenant of Abraham," as Abraham's circumcision was made the sign of his covenant with God). Circumcision is one of the basic demands of Judaism. If the father of a newly born male infant did not have him circumcised (on the eighth day), he was regarded as not fulfilling the law (once upon a time he could even be compelled by a Jewish court to have the operation performed).

Apart from the child, the chief participants in the ritual are the *mohel* (the performer of the rite), the father and the *sandek* (from the Greek *synteknos*). In our picture, the godmother is bringing the child to the door of the synagogue. The *sandek,* a local dignitary, is seated on the circumcision chair holding a pillow in his lap for the child, who will be circumcised by the mohel who stands at his side with knife poised. To the right, note the old man, with the *tefillin* on his forehead, who, entirely unconcerned, is immersed in study of the holy text.

2 PRESENTATION AT THE SYNAGOGUE

The original title of the painting is *Das Schultragen*, literally, carrying the child to the synagogue. The ceremony was practiced mostly in German synagogues. The little boy, aged one to three, is taken to the synagogue to present his *Wimpel*—the swaddling cloth used during circumcision, which was cut into three or four pieces, and stitched together to make a Torah binder. The *Wimpel* was formally presented on the child's first visit to the synagogue. Embroidered and later painted on the *Wimpel* was the name of the boy, the date of his birth and the standard formula: "May the Lord raise him up to the study of Torah, to the nuptial canopy and to good deeds." The child is taking part in the synagogue ceremony as the father helps him to touch the "trees of life," as the Torah staves are called, in fulfillment of the saying: "Torah is a tree of life to them that lay hold of it."

3   THE RABBI'S BLESSING

After the Sabbath service the boy, accompanied by his father, approaches the venerable rabbi for his blessing. This is clearly a traditional rabbi, who, while he conducts all the services in the synagogue, is primarily a scholar (see the large open book before him). The scene takes place between the *almemor* (the raised section on which the reading-desk is situated) and the *aron kodesh* (the Torah Ark, in which the Torah scrolls are kept). Note the *ner tamid*, or Eternal Light, the lamp that is kept burning in the synagogue in memory of the light that "burned continually" in front of the desert Tabernacle (Exodus 27:20-21). On the curtain *(parokhet)* are the words of the Decalogue, "Remember the Sabbath and keep it holy." Notice also the massive *menorah* (lampstand) and the flickering candles, the *Jahrzeit* lights. Though the service is over, a pious old man continues to read his prayer book.

4 THE EXAMINATION

A learned man—a rabbi, or a teacher—listens while the boy recites what he has learned during the week in the *heder* (the elementary school for Jewish children in Europe). The gentleman's beautiful daughter carries on her lap a plate, covered with fruit, which will be given as a reward to the little scholar after he is through with his performances. Note the *Judenstern* (Jewish star) hanging from the ceiling (Christian chroniclers often mention it as a uniquely Jewish lighting fixture used on the Sabbath).

5   THE BAR-MITZVAH DISCOURSE

On the first occasion that the Torah is read following a boy's thirteenth birthday, the youngster is called up at his synagogue to the reading of the Torah, thus demonstrating his new role as a full-fledged member of the community. The teenager is tutored by a learned man to deliver a *derashah* (Talmudic discourse). Here, the boy is giving the speech in the family's living room. It is an upper-middle-class family—notice the costly clothing worn by the boy, his parents, relatives and friends. Books, pictures—including one of King Frederick the Great of Prussia—and a fine rug can be observed. After the speech, the meal will be served by the domestic. Typical of the German home scene are the two cats on the lower left.

6 THE WEDDING

The ceremony takes place under the open sky. Yet bride and bridegroom stand under a canopy *(huppah)*, their heads covered with a single prayer shawl. While the rabbi recites the blessings, the groom places a gold ring on the first finger of the bride's right hand, saying, "With this ring are you consecrated unto me according to the laws of Moses and Israel." Next to the couple are a father and a mother. The *huppah* is held by boys.

While the rabbi, covered by the *tallit* (prayer shawl) wears the Polish *streimel* (fur hat), the other men have fashionable three-cornered hats, knee-breeches and buckled shoes. In the background, on the wooden structure, are the merry-makers, the *Huppah Schlemiel* (in a harlequin's jacket) and, a few steps below, the fiddler, both of them hired to entertain the crowd. Wine is held in readiness. At the conclusion of the service, the glass of wine is thrown at the tablet with the Magen David, as popular belief held that demons could be thwarted by this practice. According to tradition, the breaking of the glass was a reminder of the destruction of the Jerusalem Temple.

7 USHERING IN THE SABBATH

The mistress of the house kindles the two lights in the *Judenstern* (the special Sabbath lamp), in order to welcome Queen Sabbath. The *Judenstern* could be lowered (by means of the saw-tooth attachment suspended from the ceiling) and thus gave rise to the popular Sabbath saying: "Lamp' herunter, Sorg' hinauf" ("Lamp down, worry up").

Note the double portion of bread (known as *hallot* or *berches*), covered as required, the wine beaker and on a server on the left, you will see the fish. On the eastern wall hangs a framed tablet known as a *mizrah* to indicate, for purposes of prayer, the direction of Jerusalem.

The father, with his watch in hand, anxiously awaits the time of departure for the synagogue, holding his impatient young son by the hand.

8 SABBATH EVE AT HOME

Returned from the synagogue, the children rush toward their father to receive his blessing. It is a large family—the sixth child is a baby, held by the mother on her lap. Undoubtedly, this is a well-to-do family. But even poorer families never failed to invite to the Friday meal an impecunious stranger. He is represented here by a young man in an outlandish coat, probably a Talmudic student from the East. He is being watched with curiosity by the boy next to the master of the house.

10 SABBATH REST

In the early decades of the nineteenth century, anti-Semitic outbursts of a violent nature were rare, at least in Central Europe. Hence, the denizens of the Jewish sections were not afraid to sit outside their houses, so unlike the Jews of Russia and Poland, who always worried about *pogromchiks*. The same narrow street, which was extremely busy during the weekdays, was perfectly quiet on a Sabbath. All shops—like the *Warenhaus von Abraham Isaak Jacobsohn & Co*—were closed. The trio in front of the closed door consists of grandmother, who must use a magnifying glass in order to read her book; her son, the slightly obese owner of the shop, and his young son. Even the cat knows that it is Sabbath, and therefore time for resting.

11 THE CONCLUSION OF THE SABBATH

In the center is the *havdalah* (separation) ceremony, which consists of a blessing recited over wine, spices, and light at the termination of the Sabbath. As the *kiddush* prayer ushers in the Sabbath, so the *havdalah* bids it farewell. Here, the father is pouring wine into a cup. All members of the family are watching him with profound attention. The blessing, which refers to the distinction between the holy and the profane, between lightness and darkness, Israel and other peoples, emphasizes the end of quiet and repose, and the start of a week of hard work for all.

12   PURIM

Purim (Lots) is a cheerful festival, since it commemorates the rescue of a group of Jews in Persia through a romantic sequence of events. Hence, it is not astonishing that all kinds of frolic was permitted during the feast's observance at home. Here, one notes a few figures coming in through the door to perform some sort of *Purim-Spiel*. It is believed that this tradition of masked, instrument-playing Purim players may very well go back to Renaissance Italy, where Jews observed and imitated the carnival practice of the Lenten season, which occurs about the time of Purim. From Italy, the custom of the *Purim-Spiel* spread to all countries where Jews were living.

13   THE PASSOVER SEDER

The father, in the center, wears the *kittel* or *sargenes*, the white garment worn by the person who is conducting the seder service on the Passover eve (white stands for purity, for the forgiveness of sins; it is the selfsame garment in which every Orthodox Jew is buried). He faces the *oreah*, the poor stranger invited to the meal. The end of the meal is in sight, for the third cup has been emptied, the son has just opened the door, through which the prophet Elijah may come (tradition-ally, a glass of wine is poured for him and placed on the table but not drunk). Soon all ceremonies will be ended, with the expression of the hope that in the year to follow the service can be held at Jerusalem.

15 YOM KIPPUR EVE

On this evening, the eve of the Day of Atonement, the *Kol Nidre*, the formula for the annulment of vows, will be recited. This is, of course, a solemn occasion, yet the picture exudes an atmosphere of peaceful contemplation rather than deep mourning. Husband and wife affectionately separate at the door of the synagogue; the wife is about to ascend to the women's section in the gallery. Traditional custom prescribed the wearing of the white garment (*kittel* or *sargenes*) and the sandals.

Note the candles on either side of the open door. To the right, two men shake hands in the spirit of good friendship and forgiveness; to the left, a grandson devotedly kisses the hand of his grandfather. At the other end of the street, the steeple of a church is noticeable; at the time the picture was painted, Christianity and Judaism had buried their hostilities, and all men of good will were ready to participate in the good life guaranteed by an era of prosperity.

16 SUKKOT

No *Sukkot* (Feast of Tabernacles) without a *sukkah!* "Throughout the seven days and nights of the festival, the *sukkah* must be regarded as one's principal abode, and the house merely a temporary residence." The family partakes of the meals and recites prayers in the *sukkah*. The *sukkah* symbolically reminds the Jew of the divine protection afforded his ancestors when they dwelt in booths during their desert wanderings (Leviticus 23:42). The decoration of fruits and vegetables emphasizes the fact that *Sukkot* is a festival of thanksgiving for the abundance of the harvest (Deuteronomy 16:13–15). A special *sukkah* tablet can be seen suspended from the *sukkah* wall. The maid is bringing the major dish to the assembled family, while two curious schoolboys peer through the open door of the *sukkah*.

18   THE VILLAGE PEDDLER

The German title, *Der Dorfgeher*, explains that the man, who is now leaving his house, is an itinerant vendor of small goods. He carries his wares with him, on his back and over his arm. In the early nineteenth century, before the rapid building of railways and the growth of mail-order houses, he performed an important function as a distributor of industrial products among the rural communities. It was a strenuous job, but many of these peddlers, industrious and frugal as they were, became shopkeepers, while their sons or grandsons were the originators of mighty department stores.

In keeping with the custom, the peddler touches the *mezuzah*, the parchment scroll placed in a container and nailed to the door post on the right side of the entrance. In the background is the bread-winner's wife; the old man, rising from the bench, is probably his father (or father-in-law). The beggar, to whom the little boy gives a coin, is not missing from this rural genre scene—and neither are the chicken and the baby chicks.

20 THE VOLUNTEER'S RETURN

The young officer returns to his family from one of the battles fought by the Germans against Napoleon's army in the War of Liberation (1813–1815). He was wounded in the battle, and is wearing his right arm in a sling. It is a Saturday afternoon, and the officer, who seems to have just arrived, has violated the Jewish law that forbids travel on Saturday. The father has interrupted his reading in the large book—perhaps a volume of the Talmud?—before him, and is looking in a mixture of paternal pride and religious uneasiness at the decoration on his son's breast—for this decoration has the shape of a cross. The volunteer is, of course, the center of interest. Everybody is listening to his recital—except for the young boy, who admires the sword and the helmet in the corner.